PICTURE THIS:
SPOT-THE-DIFFERENCE
MOVIE PUZZLES

PICTURE THIS:

SPOT-THE-DIFFERENCE

MOVIE PUZZLES

FALL RIVER PRESS

New York

FALL RIVER PRESS

New York

An Imprint of Sterling Publishing
387 Park Avenue South
New York, NY 10016

This 2011 edition published by Fall River Press by arrangement with powerHouse Packaging & Supply, Inc.

Design by Lynne Yeamans

ISBN 978-1-4351-3320-4

Distributed in Canada by Sterling Publishing
c/o Canadian Manda Group, 165 Dufferin Street
Toronto, Ontario, Canada M6K 3H6
Distributed in the United Kingdom by GMC Distribution Services
Castle Place, 166 High Street, Lewes, East Sussex, England BN7 1XU
Distributed in Australia by Capricorn Link (Australia) Pty. Ltd.
P.O. Box 704, Windsor, NSW 2756, Australia

For information about custom editions, special sales, and premium and corporate purchases,
please contact Sterling Special Sales at 800-805-5489 or specialsales@sterlingpublishing.com.

Manufactured in China

2 4 6 8 10 9 7 5 3 1

www.sterlingpublishing.com

CONTENTS

INTRODUCTION

Are you ready to tackle this wickedly addictive collection of spot-the-difference movie puzzles? Before you begin, you might be pleased to know that research shows that people who do mentally challenging puzzles regularly find that it keeps their brains sharp. Spot-the-difference picture puzzles are especially good for challenging your concentration, memory, and visual skills. Here's how to do them:

Each puzzle consists of an original image and one (or more) that appears to be an exact copy of the first image, but has actually been subjected to digital alteration so that there are a number of differences from the original.

In this book, you will find two variations of the classic spot-the-difference puzzle. The first, and most common, is a single image presented next to its seeming twin, in which the second picture has multiple changes for you to find. The second variety is an original image plus three other copies; in these puzzles, there is one change to just one of the images—can you find it?

The puzzles are organized according to level of difficulty, so you can work your way from easy to mind-boggling or just open the book to a random page and do the puzzle before you. Don't get fixated on the level of difficulty though, as you may find that some of the easy puzzles have a subtle change that is not so simple to spot, while even the challenging puzzles can offer the sharp-eyed rookie success. The number of changes to find is noted at the top of the puzzle, and you can keep track using the popcorn meter: as you find each change, circle or cross out a kernel of popcorn.

When you're ready to discover how you've fared, turn to the answer section, starting on page 117. The answer key shows the picture with the changes circled and numbered with a corresponding explanation of the change.

Here is a practice puzzle with answer key. Look for the changes, and when you think you have found them all, check your results against the answers.

Good luck!

PUZZLE #40

1. Shadow added. **2.** Flame missing. **3.** Tassle missing. **4.** Wood missing. **5.** Hairdo altered. **6.** Bottletop added. **7.** Tassle missing. **8.** Folds missing. **9.** Pattern altered. **10.** Bulb missing.

1 THE BREAKFAST CLUB

John Hughes, 1985.

KEEP SCORE:

PICTURED: Judd Nelson, Emilio Estevez, Ally Sheedy, Molly Ringwald, Anthony Michael Hall

Tim Burton, 1990.

KEEP SCORE:

PICTURED: Johnny Depp

Joel and Ethan Coen, 1987.

KEEP SCORE:    PICTURED: Holly Hunter

4 MR. MOM

EASY | 7 CHANGES

ANSWERS ON PAGE 117

Stan Dragoti, 1983.

KEEP SCORE:    **PICTURED:** Brittany/Courtney White, Michael Keaton

Alexander Payne, 1999.

KEEP SCORE:

PICTURED: Matthew Broderick, Reese Witherspoon

TRACY FLICK FOR PRESIDENT! SIGN UP FOR TODAY TOMORROW!

6 WEIRD SCIENCE

EASY | **1 CHANGE**

ANSWERS ON PAGE 117

John Hughes, 1985.

KEEP SCORE:

PICTURED: Kelly LeBrock, Anthony Michael Hall

DO THE RIGHT THING

EASY | 1 CHANGE

ANSWERS ON PAGE 118

Spike Lee, 1989.

KEEP SCORE:    **PICTURED:** Richard Edson, Spike Lee

Steven Spielberg, 1975.

KEEP SCORE:

PICTURED: Richard Dreyfuss

Jonathan Demme, 1991.

KEEP SCORE:    PICTURED: Anthony Hopkins

10 HELL ON FRISCO BAY

EASY | 7 CHANGES

ANSWERS ON PAGE 118

Frank Tuttle, 1955.

KEEP SCORE:

PICTURED: Edward G. Robinson, Joanne Dru

HAROLD AND KUMAR GO TO WHITE CASTLE

Danny Leiner, 2004.

KEEP SCORE:

PICTURED: Kal Penn, John Cho, Malin Akerman

EASY | 8 CHANGES

ANSWERS ON PAGE 118

John Lafia, 1990.

KEEP SCORE:

PICTURED: Alex Vincent, Chuckie

13 RAGING BULL

EASY | 8 CHANGES

ANSWERS ON PAGE 119

Martin Scorsese, 1980.

KEEP SCORE:    **PICTURED:** Robert De Niro, Joe Pesci

14 CLASS OF 1984

Mark L. Lester, 1982.

KEEP SCORE:

PICTURED: Lisa Langlois, Timothy Van Patten, Stefan Arngrim, Neil Clifford, Keith Knight

Sam Mendes, 1999.

KEEP SCORE:    PICTURED: Kevin Spacey

Tim Burton, 1985.

KEEP SCORE:

PICTURED: Paul Reubens

Tobe Hooper, 1982.

EASY | 8 CHANGES

ANSWERS ON PAGE 119

KEEP SCORE:

PICTURED: Craig T. Nelson, Heather O'Rourke, JoBeth Williams

18 TO SIR, WITH LOVE

EASY | 8 CHANGES

ANSWERS ON PAGE 119

James Clavell, 1967.

KEEP SCORE:

PICTURED: Richard Willson, Sidney Poitier, Christopher Chittell, Lulu

19 WILLY WONKA & THE CHOCOLATE FACTORY

EASY | **8 CHANGES**

ANSWERS ON PAGE 120

Mel Stuart, 1971.

KEEP SCORE:

PICTURED: Gene Wilder

Quentin Tarantino, 1994.

KEEP SCORE:

PICTURED: Uma Thurman, John Travolta

Steve Barron, 1990.

KEEP SCORE:

PICTURED: Raphael, Leonardo, Michelangelo, Donatello

22 SPEEDWAY

Norman Taurog, 1968.

KEEP SCORE:    PICTURED: Elvis Presley

23 VIDEODROME

David Cronenberg, 1983.

KEEP SCORE:

PICTURED: James Woods, Deborah Harry

John Landis, 1983.

KEEP SCORE:

PICTURED: Don Ameche, Eddie Murphy, Ralph Bellamy

Don Siegel, 1970.

KEEP SCORE:

PICTURED: Alberto Morin, Shirley MacLaine, Clint Eastwood

François Truffaut, 1966.

KEEP SCORE:  **PICTURED:** Julie Christie

James W. Horne, Leo McCarey, 1929.

KEEP SCORE:

PICTURED: Stan Laurel, Oliver Hardy

Tim Burton, 1988.

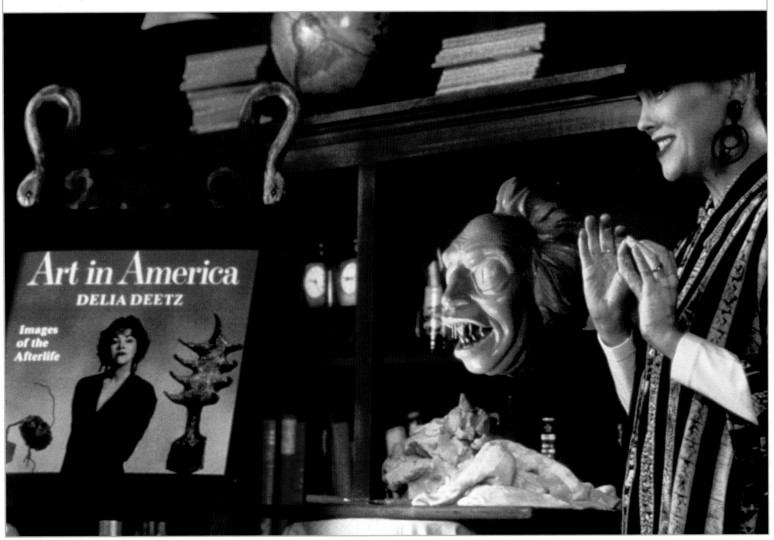

KEEP SCORE:

PICTURED: Catherine O'Hara

Brian De Palma, 1974.

KEEP SCORE:

PICTURED: William Finley, Paul Williams

Stephen Daldry, 2000.

KEEP SCORE:    PICTURED: Jamie Bell

31 | SPIDER-MAN 2

Sam Raimi, 2004.

KEEP SCORE:    PICTURED: Tobey Maguire

Howard Deutch, 1986.

KEEP SCORE:

PICTURED: Jon Cryer, Molly Ringwald

John Badham, 1977.

KEEP SCORE:    **PICTURED:** John Travolta

Michael Ritchie, 1976.

KEEP SCORE:  **PICTURED:** Walter Matthau

Ridley Scott, 1991.

KEEP SCORE:

PICTURED: Susan Sarandon, Geena Davis

Tim Burton, 1989.

KEEP SCORE:

PICTURED: Jack Nicholson

AUSTIN POWERS: THE SPY WHO SHAGGED ME

Jay Roach, 1999.

KEEP SCORE:

PICTURED: Verne Troyer, Mike Myers

Frank Tashlin, 1956.

KEEP SCORE:

PICTURED: Tom Ewell, Jayne Mansfield

Danny Boyle, 1996.

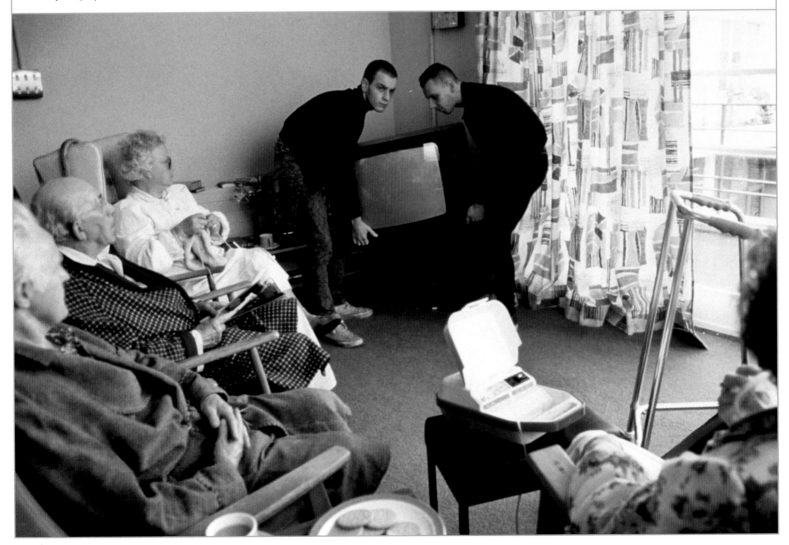

KEEP SCORE:

PICTURED: Ewan McGregor, Ewen Bremner

Mel Brooks, 1974.

KEEP SCORE:

PICTURED: Madeline Kahn, Peter Boyle

41 THE MAGIC CHRISTIAN

MEDIUM | 10 CHANGES

ANSWERS ON PAGE 123

Joseph McGrath, 1969.

KEEP SCORE:  PICTURED: Peter Sellers

42 | BIG

MEDIUM | 10 CHANGES

ANSWERS ON PAGE 123

Penny Marshall, 1988.

KEEP SCORE:    PICTURED: Tom Hanks

David Gordon Green, 2008.

KEEP SCORE:

PICTURED: Seth Rogen, James Franco, Danny McBride

John Waters, 1988.

John G. Avildsen, 1981.

KEEP SCORE: PICTURED: Dan Aykroyd, John Belushi

46	**CADDYSHACK**		MEDIUM	1 CHANGE

ANSWERS ON PAGE 124

Harold Ramis, 1980.

KEEP SCORE:

PICTURED: Michael O'Keefe, Chevy Chase, Bill Murray

Woody Allen, 1977.

KEEP SCORE:

PICTURED: Woody Allen, Diane Keaton

DINO DE LAURENTIIS PRESENTS
INGRID BERGMAN'S
"FACE TO FACE"
Starring
LIV ULLMANN
...ected and Produced by INGMAR BERGMAN   Filmed in Color by SVEN ...
A Paramount Release

Robert Luketic, 2001.

KEEP SCORE:

PICTURED: Alanna Ubach, Reese Witherspoon, Jessica Cauffiel

MEDIUM | **10 CHANGES**

ANSWERS ON PAGE 125

John "Bud" Cardos, 1977.

KEEP SCORE:    **PICTURED:** Altovise Davis

Bobby and Peter Farrelly, 1996.

MEDIUM | 10 CHANGES

ANSWERS ON PAGE 125

KEEP SCORE: 🎳🎳🎳🎳🎳🎳🎳🎳🎳🎳

PICTURED: Woody Harrelson

Kevin Smith, 2006.

KEEP SCORE:

PICTURED: Jeff Anderson, Trevor Fehrman, Brian O'Halloran

John Landis, 1978

KEEP SCORE:

PICTURED: Bruce McGill, James Widdoes, Stephen Furst, Tom Hulce, John Belushi

Julien Temple, 1986.

KEEP SCORE: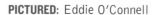

PICTURED: Eddie O'Connell

KEEP SCORE:

PICTURED: John Cusack, Chuck Mitchell

John Glen, 1981.

KEEP SCORE:

PICTURED: Desmond Llewelyn, Roger Moore

CROUCHING TIGER, HIDDEN DRAGON

Ang Lee, 2000.

KEEP SCORE: 　　　　　　**PICTURED:** Michelle Yeoh

KEEP SCORE:

PICTURED: Harrison Ford, Edward James Olmos

Ken Kwapis, 1985.

KEEP SCORE:

PICTURED: Big Bird (Caroll Spinney), Snuffleupagus (Martin Robinson)

Betty Thomas, 1995.

KEEP SCORE:

PICTURED: Olivia Hack, Jennifer Elise Cox, Christopher Daniel Barnes, Shelley Long, Jesse Lee, Gary Cole, Henriette Mantel, Christine Taylor, Paul Sutera

Frank Oz, 1986.

KEEP SCORE:

PICTURED: John Candy, Rick Moranis

Roger Corman, 1961.

KEEP SCORE:

PICTURED: Barbara Steele, Vincent Price

KEEP SCORE:

PICTURED: Arnold Schwarzenegger

Alan Arkush, 1979.

KEEP SCORE:

PICTURED: Johnny Ramone, Marky Ramone, P.J. Soles, Joey Ramone, Dee Dee Ramone

Pete Docter, David Silverman, Lee Unkrich, 2001.

KEEP SCORE:

STANDBY

GONE WITH THE WIND

Victor Fleming, 1939.

KEEP SCORE: **PICTURED:** Clark Gable, Vivien Leigh

66 HIGH FIDELITY

HARD | 12 CHANGES

ANSWERS ON PAGE 127

Stephen Frears, 2000.

KEEP SCORE:  **PICTURED:** John Cusack, Jack Black

Harold Ramis, 1983.

KEEP SCORE:

PICTURED: Chevy Chase, Anthony Michael Hall, Beverly D'Angelo, Dana Barron

Richard Donner, 1985.

KEEP SCORE:

PICTURED: Corey Feldman, Sean Astin, Jeff Cohen

Francis Ford Coppola, 1983.

KEEP SCORE:

PICTURED: Ralph Macchio, Tom Cruise, C. Thomas Howell, Rob Lowe, Matt Dillon

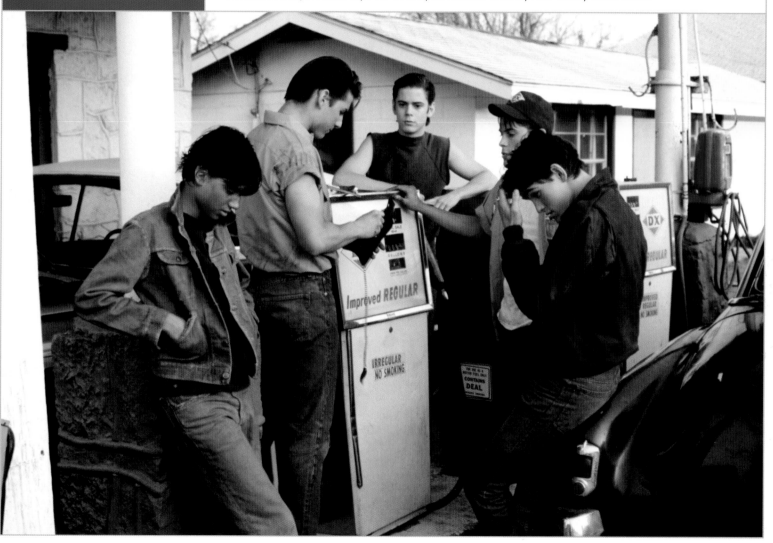

Michael Schultz, 1978.

PICTURED: Robin Gibb, Peter Frampton, George Burns, Maurice Gibb, Barry Gibb

71 THE BOURNE IDENTITY

HARD | 12 CHANGES

ANSWERS ON PAGE 128

Doug Liman, 2002.

KEEP SCORE:  **PICTURED:** Matt Damon

ANSWERS 1-6

PUZZLE #1

1. Railing missing. **2.** Bandana missing. **3.** Smoke missing. **4.** Tank top color changed. **5.** Logo missing. **6.** Pants color changed. **7.** Magazines shuffled.

PUZZLE #2

1. Shadow missing. **2.** Wire missing. **3.** Metal rings added. **4.** Word misspelled. **5.** Scissors missing. **6.** Photo added. **7.** Object color changed.

PUZZLE #3

1. Metal piece missing. **2.** Metal piece moved left. **3.** Wings flopped. **4.** Metal piece missing. **5.** Name missing. **6.** Metal bar missing. **7.** Badge moved down.

PUZZLE #4

1. Part of curtain missing. **2.** Red stripe missing. **3.** Ring missing. **4.** Spinner rotated. **5.** Button missing. **6.** Hole missing. **7.** Stripe missing.

PUZZLE #5

1. Fire extinguisher missing. **2.** Briefcase missing. **3.** Tie stripes altered. **4.** Text altered. **5.** Color changed. **6.** Head added. **7.** Barrette missing.

PUZZLE #6

Top right puzzle: Bracelet missing.

ANSWERS 7-12

PUZZLE #7
Bottom right puzzle: Numbers missing.

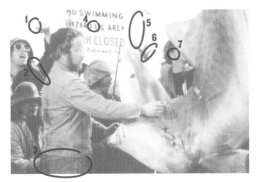

PUZZLE #8
1. Finger bent. **2.** Arrow added. **3.** Pants color changed. **4.** Letter missing. **5.** Pole missing. **6.** Stake added. **7.** Sideburn missing.

PUZZLE #9
1. Paper missing. **2.** Shirt color changed. **3.** Drawing altered. **4.** Piece missing. **5.** Artwork missing. **6.** Artwork flopped. **7.** Stones merged.

PUZZLE #10
1. Forehead shortened. **2.** Tie color altered. **3.** Gun missing. **4.** Scarf decorations added. **5.** Chimney added. **6.** Window added. **7.** Color changed.

PUZZLE #11
1. Mouth altered. **2.** Painting altered. **3.** Tongue missing. **4.** Buckle missing. **5.** Pom poms missing. **6.** Curtain color changed. **7.** Part of window ledge missing. **8.** Rip in jeans missing.

PUZZLE #12
1. Buttons switched. **2.** Mouth altered. **3.** Stripe color changed. **4.** Eyebrow missing. **5.** Button added. **6.** Watch altered. **7.** Hat pattern added. **8.** Stripes missing.

ANSWERS 13-18

PUZZLE #13

1. Head missing. **2.** Chest hair missing. **3.** Belt moved up. **4a and 4b.** Stripe color changed. **5.** Sideburn lengthened. **6.** Bowtie color changed. **7.** Hand missing. **8.** Paper in pocket added.

PUZZLE #14

1. Necklace missing. **2.** Mask changed. **3.** Mouth changed. **4.** Ear missing. **5.** Nailpolish added. **6.** Metal spikes added. **7.** Stripe color changed. **8.** Handle missing.

PUZZLE #15

Top left puzzle: Headset missing.

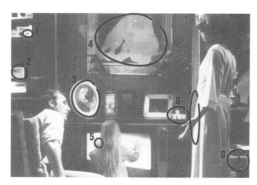

PUZZLE #16

Bottom left puzzle: Pocket kerchief altered.

PUZZLE #17

1. Buttons added. **2.** Stereo added. **3.** Picture changed. **4.** Picture flopped. **5.** Finger added. **6.** Blocks moved right. **7.** Belt removed. **8.** Color changed.

PUZZLE #18

1. Poster changed. **2.** Tie stripes color changed. **3.** Bottle added. **4.** Bowl color changed. **5.** Handle moved. **6.** Hair color changed. **7.** Utensil added. **8.** Word changed.

ANSWERS 19-24

PUZZLE #19

1. Dot missing. **2.** Dot missing. **3.** Light added. **4.** Bowtie color changed. **5.** Ceiling altered. **6.** Flower petal missing. **7.** Dot missing. **8.** Dot missing.

PUZZLE #20

1. Bartender missing. **2.** Letter added. **3.** Pole added. **4.** Globe added. **5.** Type flopped. **6.** Pants color changed. **7.** Number changed. **8.** Rocks altered.

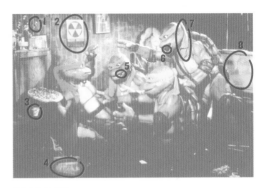

PUZZLE #21

1. Garland added. **2.** Poster flopped. **3.** Cup color changed. **4.** Newspaper added. **5.** Tooth missing. **6.** Tongue missing. **7.** Bandana color changed. **8.** Television screen picture added.

PUZZLE #22

1. Sign color changed. **2.** Line of "E" missing. **3.** Cars in photo missing. **4.** Headlight missing. **5.** Harmonica missing. **6.** Guitar color changed. **7.** Guitar stem missing. **8.** Stripe missing.

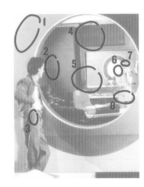

PUZZLE #23

1. Wall line moved. **2.** Reflection missing. **3.** Pocket missing. **4.** Board extended. **5.** Lamp missing. **6.** Head missing. **7.** Headband color changed. **8.** Skirt pattern altered.

PUZZLE #24

1. Painting missing. **2.** Painting altered. **3.** Flower added. **4.** Metal piece added. **5.** Cuff missing. **6.** Orange juice lowered. **7.** Tie pattern altered. **8.** Computer screen blue bar missing. **9.** Coffee missing.

ANSWERS 25-30

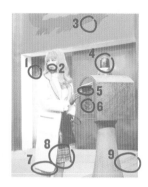

PUZZLE #25
I. Flames taller. **2.** Shelf raised. **3.** Cross lengthened. **4.** Brandy drunk. **5.** Glass added. **6.** Stick missing. **7.** Belt missing. **8.** Medal moved right. **9.** Ribbon missing.

PUZZLE #26
I. Shadow altered. **2.** Lipstick color changed. **3.** Foot missing. **4.** Light color changed. **5.** Letter missing. **6.** Dragon flopped. **7.** Coat lengthened. **8.** Skirt color changed. **9.** Line in sidewalk added.

PUZZLE #27
I. Branches added. **2.** Hinge missing. **3.** Tie color changed. **4.** Tree missing. **5.** Window missing. **6.** Hood ornament added. **7.** Grille added. **8.** Vent added. **9.** Shadow missing.

PUZZLE #28
I. Continent flopped. **2.** Magazines missing. **3.** Text changed. **4.** Text changed. **5.** Character switched. **6.** Book added. **7.** Teeth color changed. **8.** Spine color changed. **9.** Earring larger.

PUZZLE #29
I. Panel missing. **2.** Buttons missing. **3.** Knob missing. **4.** Eyehole missing. **5.** Buttons missing. **6.** Eyeglasses color changed. **7.** Piano keys missing. **8.** Stripe missing. **9.** Ring missing.

PUZZLE #30
I. Stripe added. **2.** Ribbon missing. **3.** Window lowered. **4.** Pole extended. **5.** Sock lengthened. **6.** Black brick missing. **7.** Outlet moved right. **8.** Leaf missing. **9.** Grass added.

ANSWERS 31-36

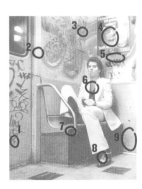

PUZZLE #31

1. Ornament moved. **2.** Building narrowed. **3.** Eye color changed. **4.** Leg missing. **5.** Top of building missing. **6.** Row of windows added. **7.** Bar missing. **8.** Shadow added. **9.** Bar added.

PUZZLE #32

1. Text altered. **2.** Flower color changed. **3.** Stripes color changed. **4.** Bracelet missing. **5.** Window widened. **6.** Picture changed. **7.** Flower added. **8.** Picture changed. **9.** Watch moved down.

PUZZLE #33

1. Arrow added. **2.** Bolts added. **3.** Bolt added. **4.** Drink color changed. **5.** Paint filled in red. **6.** Necklaces missing. **7.** Metal piece missing. **8.** Piece of shoelace added. **9.** Metal panel missing.

PUZZLE #34

1. Patch added. **2.** Text altered. **3.** Leaves altered. **4.** Stripe missing. **5.** Text altered. **6.** Number missing. **7.** Leg missing. **8.** Sock color filled in yellow. **9.** Type on label missing.

PUZZLE #35

1. Mountaintop altered. **2.** Bracelet missing. **3.** Metal belt piece missing. **4.** Rock added. **5.** Mountain range missing. **6.** Tumbleweed added. **7.** Cylinder missing. **8.** Number changed. **9.** Pole added.

PUZZLE #36

Bottom right puzzle: Bird missing.

ANSWERS 37-42

PUZZLE #37

Top left puzzle: Cat's tail missing.

PUZZLE #38

1. Light added. **2.** Head added. **3.** Hand missing. **4.** Earrings missing. **5.** Flower missing. **6.** Pattern altered. **7.** Pocket moved down. **8.** Light fixture added. **9.** Glass missing. **10.** Cigarette missing.

PUZZLE #39

1. Cane missing. **2.** Cup color changed. **3.** Television picture changed. **4.** Box moved left. **5.** Stripes missing. **6.** Pattern switched. **7.** Rail added. **8.** Coffee color changed. **9.** Cookie added. **10.** Tube missing.

PUZZLE #40

1. Shadow added. **2.** Flame missing. **3.** Tassle missing. **4.** Wood missing. **5.** Hairdo altered. **6.** Bottletop added. **7.** Tassle missing. **8.** Folds missing. **9.** Pattern altered. **10.** Bulb missing.

PUZZLE #41

1. Books color changed. **2.** Pole missing. **3.** Black bar added to spine of book. **4.** Inner circle missing. **5.** Stripes missing. **6.** Circle color changed. **7.** Knob added. **8.** Pipe extended. **9.** Knob moved down. **10.** Picture moved right.

PUZZLE #42

1. Yellow added. **2.** Giraffe head missing. **3.** Head missing. **4.** Stripe color changed. **5.** Pattern altered. **6.** Shoe color changed. **7.** Piano keys moved left. **8.** Art on bag missing. **9.** Watch missing. **10.** Lamp altered.

ANSWERS 43-48

PUZZLE #43
1. Flowers added. **2.** Wristband added. **3.** Yellow stripe missing. **4.** Reflector added. **5.** Stripes color changed. **6.** Hill added. **7.** Road sign missing. **8.** Necklace missing. **9.** Reg flag raised. **10.** Shoe switched.

PUZZLE #44
1. Light added. **2.** Earring missing. **3.** Wig color changed. **4.** Branches added. **5.** Nozzle missing. **6.** Red dot added. **7.** Piece of bracelet missing. **8.** Bracelet added. **9.** Frame altered. **10.** Letter changed.

PUZZLE #45
Top right puzzle: Cigar missing.

PUZZLE #46
Bottom left puzzle: Golf club missing.

PUZZLE #47
1. Reflection added. **2.** Line missing. **3.** Buttonhole missing. **4.** Collar color changed. **5.** Button moved up. **6.** Ring added. **7.** Piece of ribbon missing. **8.** Word changed. **9.** Pattern altered. **10.** Outline missing.

PUZZLE #48
1. Flowers added. **2.** Button moved. **3.** Middle of "U" filled in. **4.** Word missing. **5.** Eye color changed. **6.** Necklace missing. **7.** Laces missing. **8.** Belt color changed. **9.** Hair lengthened. **10.** Boot missing.

ANSWERS 49-54

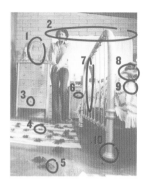

PUZZLE #49

1. Mirror missing. **2.** Curtain rod lowered. **3.** Knob added. **4.** Spider added. **5.** Leg added. **6.** Knob added. **7.** Rail missing. **8.** Blanket color changed. **9.** Pattern missing. **10.** Pole altered.

PUZZLE #50

1. Type changed. **2.** Photo missing. **3.** Glasses added. **4.** Hand missing. **5.** Bowling pin added. **6.** Ball color changed. **7.** Seat colors changed. **8.** Stripe missing. **9.** Ball added. **10.** Stripe missing.

PUZZLE #51

1. Type added. **2.** Hat band color changed. **3.** Art on poster missing. **4.** Nametag missing. **5.** Hand missing. **6.** Bottle missing. **7.** Eyebrows missing. **8.** T-shirt missing. **9.** Goatee missing. **10.** Type on box missing. **11.** Apostrophe missing.

PUZZLE #52

1. Bowtie missing. **2.** Photo changed. **3.** Magazines color changed. **4.** Pencil added. **5.** Glass missing. **6.** Photo changed. **7.** Belt missing. **8.** Sand added. **9.** Pattern rotated. **10.** Knob missing. **11.** Pencils missing.

PUZZLE #53

1. Text changed. **2.** Neon sign color changed. **3.** Musical note added. **4.** Mustache added. **5.** Lamp added. **6.** Watch missing. **7.** Person missing. **8.** Image added in mirror. **9.** Bottle added. **10.** Wall sconce missing. **11.** Light lengthened.

PUZZLE #54

1a and 1b. Ears flopped. **2.** Eyes moved up. **3.** Bracket added. **4.** Stack taller. **5.** Cigar moved to John's mouth. **6a and 6b.** Stripes added. **7.** Button missing. **8.** Text missing. **9.** Food color changed. **10.** Coffee added. **11.** Faucet missing.

ANSWERS 55-60

PUZZLE #55

Top right puzzle: Spokes added.

PUZZLE #56

Top left puzzle: Buns added.

PUZZLE #57

1. Bottle switched. **2.** Badge moved left. **3.** Liquid missing. **4.** Food added. **5.** Part of mustache missing. **6.** Pattern rotated. **7.** Chopsticks added. **8.** Vest color changed. **9.** Handle missing. **10.** Stripe missing. **11.** Knob missing.

PUZZLE #58

1. Hole missing. **2.** Tail missing. **3.** Art missing. **4.** Tie added. **5.** Flowers changed color. **6.** Beads added. **7.** Clock missing. **8.** Blanket color changed. **9.** Flag missing. **10.** Beads changed. **11.** Metal piece moved.

PUZZLE #59

1. Word missing. **2.** Paper towel roll smaller. **3.** Hinge added. **4.** Blender and outlet moved right. **5.** Tie missing. **6.** Utensil added. **7.** Cup added. **8.** Pockets color changed. **9.** Nozzle lengthened. **10.** Orange juice higher. **11.** Pancake missing.

PUZZLE #60

1. Paper missing. **2.** Number and question mark missing. **3.** Text missing. **4.** Jar missing. **5.** Flower added. **6.** Paper missing. **7.** Business card added. **8.** Cup taller. **9.** Microphone lengthened. **10.** Bandage added. **11.** Knob missing. **12.** Condiments added.

ANSWERS 61-66

PUZZLE #61

1. Candle missing. **2.** Finial missing. **3.** Decoration added. **4.** Ring missing. **5.** Pattern flopped. **6.** Grass missing. **7.** Head missing. **8.** Ruffle shortened. **9.** Glass color changed. **10.** Fringe added. **11.** Brushes missing. **12.** Fringe color changed.

PUZZLE #62

1. Light missing. **2.** Collar missing. **3.** Woman missing. **4.** Letter added. **5.** Head missing. **6.** Light added. **7.** Light added. **8.** Orange stripe added. **9.** Metal piece added. **10.** Belt buckle missing. **11.** Pants color changed. **12.** Text changed.

PUZZLE #63

1. Light missing. **2.** Graffiti number 8 missing. **3.** Logo missing. **4.** Head missing. **5.** Letter switched. **6.** Stripe color changed. **7.** Letters switched. **8.** Letters missing. **9.** Fret missing. **10.** Holes in pants missing. **11.** Stripes added. **12.** Circle missing.

PUZZLE #64

1. Logo flopped. **2.** Horns color changed. **3.** Words moved. **4.** Numbers "12" and "6" on clock switched. **5.** Lever flipped to the other side of bell. **6.** Hat added. **7.** Tooth missing. **8.** Eye color changed. **9.** Eye added. **10.** Spike added. **11.** Monster moved left. **12.** Toe added.

PUZZLE #65

1. Piece of garland missing. **2.** Photo changed. **3.** Leaf missing. **4.** Star added. **5.** Tie missing. **6.** Instrument missing. **7.** Photo changed. **8.** Ruffle color changed. **9.** Head added. **10.** Sideburn missing. **11.** Bow color changed. **12.** Cuff missing.

PUZZLE #66

1. Disk added. **2.** Boxes missing. **3.** Sticker changed. **4.** Shelf of CDs switched. **5.** CDs missing. **6.** Words missing. **7.** Object missing. **8.** Art flopped. **9.** Word missing. **10.** Baby flopped. **11.** Sleeves added. **12.** Tab missing.

ANSWERS 67-71

PUZZLE #67

1. Leaves added. **2.** Bar added. **3.** Fingers moved. **4.** Alligator logo missing. **5.** Button added. **6.** Stripe added. **7.** Flower added. **8.** Sleeping bag added. **9.** Suitcase flopped. **10.** Steering wheel missing. **11.** Handle missing. **12.** Taillights color changed.

PUZZLE #68

1. Sign filled in blue. **2.** Shirt pattern missing. **3.** Ice cream color changed. **4.** Lids color changed. **5.** Letters switched. **6.** Can added. **7.** Soda label switched. **8.** Word missing. **9.** Shirt color changed. **10.** Word changed. **11.** Batteries added. **12.** Flowers added.

PUZZLE #69

1. Bar moved left. **2.** Bumps in wall missing. **3.** Tattoo missing. **4.** Chain lengthened. **5.** Text changed. **6.** Text changed. **7.** Hat color changed. **8.** Words missing. **9.** Triangles added. **10.** Hose added. **11.** Knob missing. **12.** Metal piece missing.

PUZZLE #70

1. Window missing. **2.** Text changed. **3.** Head added. **4.** Decoration missing. **5.** Pockets missing. **6.** Symbol changed. **7.** Mustard color changed. **8.** Hair shortened. **9.** Decoration missing. **10.** Row of windows added. **11.** Blue sequins and white star added. **12.** Leg added.

PUZZLE #71

1. Flag color changed. **2.** Window missing. **3.** Letter changed. **4.** Pole added. **5.** Sign added. **6.** Head missing. **7.** Strap missing. **8.** Flap missing. **9.** Zipper unzipped. **10.** Logo missing. **11.** Black strap missing. **12.** Color changed.